It is our hope that this book is extremely helpful in your day to day activities. There may be an instance or here you find that there is something not listed in this book that you wish were there. You it there is a way that this book could be more helpful to you. In either case, we are more ke your requests and suggestions into consideration for our 2nd edition. Please feel free to ments along to us.

Need Another Copy of <u>Kitchen Spanish</u>? Here's How!

out your mailing info in the spaces provided. Mail $11.95 for each book ordered
and a copy of the completed form along with
for the first book and $1 s/h for each additional copy up to $8 maximum s/h to:

Cave Brothers, Corp.   P.O.Box 220401   Great Neck, New York 11021

_____ # of Books_____

_____

_____ State _____ Zip _____

New York State residents please include appropriate sales tax.
Orders of 120 books or more shipped free in continental U.S.

If you have any suggestions for future editions of Kitchen Spanish, please feel free to send them in to:

Cave Brothers Corp.
P.O. Box 220401
Great Neck, NY 11022-0401

Kitchen Spanish

A Quick Phrase Guide of Kitchen and Culinary Terms

Updated Version

by Michael A. Friend and T. J. Loughran

CAVE BROTHERS, CORP.

Great Neck, New York

Kitchen Spanish
Published by
Cave Brothers, Corp.
P.O. Box 220401 Great Neck, NY 11021
1-516-674-2373

Copyright © 1996, 2007 by Cave Brothers, Corp.

Library of Congress Catalog Card Number 96-84316

ISBN number 0-9651901-0-2

TABLE OF CONTENTS

ACKNOWLEDGMENTS

The purpose of this book is to make it possible for non-Spanish speaking individuals to converse in usable Spanish with individuals who only speak Spanish, in a Kitchen or Hospitality work environment. We don't pretend that this book is perfect, however, we believe that you will find it extremely helpful.

The authors would like to thank the following people for their support and/or assistance in making the production of this book possible. Special thanks go to Ronald Marcellin R.I.P. who taught us everything he had learned about Spanish only two weeks earlier. We miss him. To our friends Juan, Verceli and Evelyn at Los Rancheros Restaurante, no longer in Jamaica, Queens for their assistance and excellent food. To Kathy Friend for giving us a home. To King Joseph for bringing us the Cave. To Evelyn Gordon for putting up with us. To Denis Keane at Durow's in Glendale for his co-operation and access. To Bill and Jim at Specialty Book/Studio 31 for their invaluable assistance, and most importantly, great thanks to Joe Martino for bringing the Cave Brothers back together.

To our Moms, Rita Friend and Alice Loughran, for having us. Thanks!

HOW TO USE THIS BOOK

In the left hand column, you will see the phrase or word, spelled in English. The next column lists the Spanish equivalent, spelled in Spanish. The third column will show you how to pronounce the word or phrase so that you will be understood by a Spanish speaking person. *eg.* (**Hello   ¡Hola!   OH-lah**)

In the third column, there will be one syllable in each word that is written in **UPPER CASE** letters. This is the part of the word that receives the accent. This may be said in a slightly higher pitch or maybe a little louder than the rest of the word. *eg.* (**KAHR-neh**)

In the section titled **Complex Sentences,** there are two places where you can fill in the blanks. We have provided one possible choice for each blank in the sentence. You will no doubt find yourself needing other choices. These will be found in the back of the book in the section labeled, **The Glossary**.

PRONUNCIATION GUIDE

This pronuciation guide is for use with the phonetics provided.

AY	Sound of long A as in WAY.
EE	Sound of long E as in GLEE.
G	Sounds like G in girl.
H	Sound like H in Harry
OH	Sound of long O as in NO , GO, SNOW.
OO	Sound as in MOO or BOO.
RR	Sound of a rolling R. Roll the tongue (sound of a motorboat).
SS	Indicates the sound of a hard S as in ssnake

Occasionally you will see an English word in italics preceded by a consonant
eg. SAIR, MWHERE, GLACE. Pronounce the English word as written and add the sound of
the consonant before it. It is very important (muy importante) in Hispanic culture to
speak in a polite and courteous tone. This is easily accomplished by liberal use of
Please (Por Favór) and Thank You (Grácias). **This cannot be overstressed!**

COMMON WORDS, PHRASES AND INSTRUCTIONS

Bad	mal	**mahl**
Be careful	tenga cuidado	**TEHNG-ah kwee-DAH-doh**
Blanch the vegetables	Blanquee los vegetales	**BLAHN-kay lohss veh-jeh-TAH-lehss**
Boil the water	Hierva el agua	**YEHR-vah el AH-gwah**
Clean this up	Limpia este.	**LEEM-pee-ah ESS-tay**
Clean this area	Limpia esta área	**LEEM-pee-ah ESS-tah AH-ree-ah**
Close the door	Cierra la puerta	*see-AIR*-rah lah P*WHERE* -tah
Come here	Ven aqui	**BEN ah- KEE**
Come with me	Ven conmigo	**BEN cohn-MEE-goh**
Cook this "Rare"	Coce este poco hecho	**KOH-seh EHSS-tay POH-koh EH-choh**
Cook this "Medium"	Coce este mediano	**KOH-seh EHSS-tay meh-dee-AH-noh**
Cook this "Well Done"	Coce este bien cocido	**KOH-seh EHSS-tay bee-EHN koh-SEE-doh**
do this	Haz esto	**AHZ ESS-toh**
Do this quickly	Haz esto rapido	**AHZ ESS-toh RRAH-pee-doh**
Do you have everything ready?	¿Tienes todo listo?	**tee-EH-nehss TOH-doh LEESS-toh**
Do you need help?	¿Necesitas tú ayuda?	**neh-seh-SEE-tahss too ah-YOO-deh**
Empty the garbage	Vacie la basura	**bah-see lah bah-*SUE*-rah**
Excuse me	Escusa me	**ess-SCU-sah may**

Excuse me please	Escusa me por favor	ess-SCU-sah may pour fah-VORE
Finish this later	Termina lo mas tarde	tehr-MEE-nah loh mahss *TAR*-day
Get to work	Empiezo a trabajar.	em-pee-AA-zoh ah trah-bah-HARR
Give me this quickly	Ha me esso rápido.	Ah may ESS-oh RAH-pee-doh
Good	Bueno	B*WAY* - noh
good afternoon	buenas tardes	B*WAY*-nahss TAR -dehss
Goodbye	Adios	ah-dee-OHSS
good morning	Buenas días	B*WAY*-nahss DEE-ahss
Good Work !	¡ Buen trabajo !	B*WHEN* trah-BAH-hoh
Hello	¡Hola!	OH-lah
How are you?	¿Cómo estás?	KOH-moh ess-TAHSS
How do you say in Spanish?	Que dice en Español	kay DEE-*say* ehn EHS-pahn-nyol
Hurry up	Rápidamente	RRAH-pee-dah-mehn-tay
I don't know	Yo no sé	yoh no *SAY*
I don't know anything	Yo no sé nada	yoh no *say* Nah-dah
I'm in a hurry.	Tengo prisa	TEHN-goh PREE-sah
If you have any questions, ask!	Si tienes alguna pregunta, pregunte!	
		see tee-EHN-ehss ahl-GOO-nah preh-GOON-tah, preh-GOON-tay
I'm sorry	lo siento	loh see-EHN-toh
Maybe	Posiblemente	poh-see-bleh-MEHN-tay
Never do that	Nunca haga eso	*NOON*-kah AH-gah ESS-oh
No	No	noh

English	Spanish	Pronunciation
Now	Ahora	ah-OHR-ah
Open the windows	Abra las ventanas.	AH-brah lahss behn-TAH-nahss.
Pardon me	Perdon a me	pehr-DOHN ah may
Please	por favór	*pour* fah-VORE
Punch in	Puncha la tarjeta	POON-chah lah tahr-HEH-tah
Punch out and leave	Puncha la tarjeta y tu vete	POON-chah lah tahr-HEH-tah ee too BEH-tay
Quiet	Silencio	see-LEN-see-oh
Right now	Ahora mismo	ah-ORR-ah MEESS-moh
see you later	hasta luego	AHS-tah loo-*WAY*-go
Steam the vegetables	Cocine al vapor las vegetales	koh-SEE-neh ahl vah-POUR lahss veh-jeh-TAH-lehss
Stop	Para	Pah-rah
Take this	Tome eso.	TOH-may EHSS-oh
Thank You	Gracias	GRAH-see-ahss
Turn on the lights	Encienda las luces	ehn-see-EHN-dah lahss LOO-sehss
Vacuum the rug	Aspire la alfombra	ah-SPEE-reh lah ahl-FOHM-brah
Wait here	Espera aqui	ehss-*PEAR*-ah ah-KEY
Wash your hands	lávese las manos	LAH-bey-sey lahss -MAH-nohss
We have a delivery	Tenemos una entrega	teh-NEH-mohss OON-ah ehn-TREH-gah
When?	¿Cuando?	KWAHN-doh
Yes	Sí	*see*

In the following section there are basic phrases with blanks inserted at the appropriate places. In the parenthesis, you will find a possible choice.

There are other common choices listed below. There may be other words you wish to use. Chances are good that you will find them listed in **THE GLOSSARY** at the end of the book.

If you find yourself looking up the same word all the time, feel free to make notes anywhere in the book.

This is your tool. Use it!

SIMPLE DIRECTIONS

BRING _____(THE MOP)
Traiga _____(el mop)
TRI-gah _____(el MOHP)

COMMON CHOICES

the bucket	el cubo	**ehl KOO-boh**
the chef	el cocinero	**ehl koh-see-NEHR-oh**
the glasses	los vasos	**lohss VAH-sohss**
more	más	**mahss**
the plates	los platos	**lohss PLAH-toh**
salt	sal	**sahl**
that	eso	**EH-soh**
this	esta	**EHSS-tah**
water	agua	**AHG-wah**

CHOP _____ **(THE ONIONS)**
Corte _____ (los cebollas)
KOHR-teh _____ **(lohss seh-BOH-yahss)**

COMMON CHOICES

the **carrots**	las zanahorias	lahss **sahn-ah-OH-ree-ahss**
the **celery**	el apio	ehl **ah-PEE-oh**
the **cucumber**	el pepino	ehl **peh-PEE-noh**
the **eggs**	los huevos	lohss _HWAY_ **-vohss**
the **garlic**	el ajo	ehl **AH-hoh**
the **onions**	las cebollas	lahss **seh-BOH-yahss**
the **parsley**	el perejil	ehl **peh-REH-heel**
the **pork**	la carne de cerdo	la **KAR-nay deh SEHR-doh**
the **spinach**	la espinaca	lah **ess-pee-NAH-kah**
the **steak**	la tajada	lah **tah-HAH-dah**
the **tomatoes**	el tomates	ehl **toh-MAH-tehss**
the **turnips**	los nabos	lohss **nah-BOHSS**
the **walnuts**	los nueces	lohss **new-EHZ-ess**

CLEAN _____(THE TABLE).   Use this also for 'BUS' and 'CLEAR'
Limpia _____(la mesa).
LEEM-pee-ya _____(lah MEH-sah)

COMMON CHOICES

the **bathrooms**	los baños	lohss **BAHN-yohss**
the **fish**	el pescado	ehl **pehs-KAH-doh**
the **floor**	el piso	ehl **PEE-soh**
the **kitchen**	la cocina	lah **koh-SEE-nah**
the **refrigerator**	el refrigerador	ehl **ray-frig-ehr-ah-DOHR**
the **rug**	la alfombra	lah **ahl-FOHM-brah**
the **sink**	el sumidero	ehl **soo-mee-DEHR-oh**
the **stairs**	la escalera	lah **ess-kah-LEH-rah**
the **stove**	la estufa	lah **ess-TOO-fah**
the **vegetables**	los vegetales	lohss **veh-jeh-TAH-lehs**
the **windows**	las ventana(s)	lahss **ven-TAH-nah(ss)**

COOK _____ **(THE SHRIMP)**
Coce _____ (los camarones)
KOH-seh _____(**lohss kah-mah-ROH-nehss**)

COMMON CHOICES

the **cabbage**	el repollo	ehl **ray-POH-yoh**
the **cauliflower**	el coliflor	**ehl koh-LEE-flohr**
the **French fries**	las papas fritas	lahss **PAH-pas FREE-tas**
the **ham**	el jamon	ehl **hah-MOHN**
the **lobster**	la langosta	lahss **lahn-GOH-stah**
the **shrimp**	los camarones	lohss **kah-mah-ROH-nehss**
the **soup**	la sopa	lah **SOH-pah**
the **stew**	el guisado	ehl **gwee-SAH-doh**
the **turkey**	el pavo	ehl **PAH-voh**
that	eso	**EH-soh**
them	los	**lohss**
these	estos	**EH-stohss**
this	esta	**EHSS-tah**

CUT _____(THE BREAD.)
Corta _____(el pan)
KOHR-tah _____(ehl PAHN)

COMMON CHOICES

the **carrots**	los zanahorias	lohss **sahn-ah-OH-ree-ahss**
the **cheese**	el queso	ehl **KAY-soh**
the **chicken**	el pollo	ehl **POH-yoh**
the **cake**	la torta	lah **TOHR-tah**
the **meat**	el carne	ehl **KAHR-nay**
the **paper**	el papel	ehl **pah-PEHL**
the **tomatoes**	los tomates	lohss **toh-MAH-tehss**
the **vegetables**	los vegetales	lohss **veh-jeh-TAH-lehs**

FRY _____ **(THE POTATOES)**
Frita _____ (las papas)
free-tah _____ **(lahss PAH-pahss)**

COMMON CHOICES

the **bacon**	el tocino	ehl **toh-SEE-noh**
the **chicken**	el pollo	ehl **POH-yoh**
the **eggplant**	la berenjena	lah **beh-rehn-HEE-nah**
the **eggs**	los huevos	lohss **HWAY-vohss**
the **fish**	el pescado	ehl **pehss-KAH-doh**
the **French fries**	las papas fritas	lahss **PAH-pas FREE-tas**
the **ham**	el jamon	ehl **hah-MOHN**
the **mushrooms**	los hongos	lohss **HOHN-gohs**
the **onions**	las cebollas	lahss **seh-BOH-yahss**
the **shrimp**	los camarones	lohss **kah-mah-ROH-nehss**
the **zucchini**	las calabacitas italianas	lahss **kah-lah-bah-SEE-tahs ee-tah-lee-AH-nahss**

GET CLEAN _____(GLASSES).
Traiga _____(vasos) limpios
TRI-gah _____(VAH-sohss) LEEM-pee-ohss

COMMON CHOICES

aprons	delantales	**deh-lahn-TAHL-ess**
coffee cups	tazas para café	**TAH-sahss PAH-rah kah-FAY**
dinner plates	platos de cema	**PLAH-tohss deh SEH-mah**
forks	tenedoras	**teh-neh-DOHR-ahss**
glasses	vasos	**VAH-sohss**
knives	cuchillos	**koo-CHEE-yohss**
pants	pantalones	**pahn-tah-LOH-nehss**
placemats	tapetes de mesa	**tah-PEH-tehs deh MEH-sah**
plates	platos	**PLAH-tohss**
spoons	cucharas	**koo-CHAR-ahss**
tablecloth	manteles	**mahn-TEH-less**
towels	toallas	**toh-AH-yahss**

GRILL _____(THE STEAK)

Cocido a la parilla _____(el bistec)

koh-SEE-doh ah lah pah-REE-yah _____(ehl bee-stehk)

COMMON CHOICES

the **chicken**	el pollo	ehl **POH-yoh**
the **chicken breasts**	la pechuga de pollo	lah **peh-CHEW-gah deh POH-yoh**
the **fish**	el pescado	ehl **pehss-KAH-doh**
the **halibut**	el hipogloso	ehl **ee-poh-GLOH-soh**
the **lamb**	el carne de cordero	ehl **KAR-nay deh kohr-Deh-roh**
the **meat**	el carne	ehl **KAHR-nay**
the **mushrooms**	los hongos	lohss **HOHN-gohss**
the **octopus**	el pulpo	ehl **POOL-poh**
the **onions**	las cebollas	lahss **seh-BOH-yahss**
the **pineapple**	la piña	lah **PEE-nyah**
the **sausage**	la salchicha	lah **sahl-CHEE-chah**
the **shrimp**	los camarones	lohss **kah-mah-ROH-nehss**

GIVE ME _____(an onion).
Déme _____(un cebolla).
DEH-meh _____(oon seh-BOH-yah)

COMMON CHOICES

brush	cepillo	**seh-PEE-yoh**
a **chair**	una silla	**OOH-nah SEE-ya**
coffee	café	**kah-FAY**
eggs	huevos	**H*WAY*-vohss**
ice	hielo	**ee-EH-loh**
milk	leche	**LEH-cheh**
potatoes	papas	**PAH-pas**
salt and pepper	sal y pimienta	**sahl ee pee-mee-EHN-tah**
strawberries	fresas	**FRAY-sahss**
sugar	azúcar	**ah-SOO-kahr**
toilet paper	papel hygienico	**pah-PEL ee-he-EN-ee-koh**
the **vacuum cleaner**	la aspiradora	**lah ah-spee-rah-DOHR-ah**

HEAT _____ (THE SOUP)
Calente _____(la sopa)
kah-LEHN-teh _____(lah SOH-pah)

COMMON CHOICES

the **bread**	el pan	ehl **pahn**
the **coffee**	el café	ehl **kah-FAY**
the **gravy**	la salsa	lah **SAHL-sah**
the **meat**	el carne	ehl **KAHR-nay**
the **oven**	el horno	ehl **OHR-noh**
the **pan**	el sartén	ehl **sahr-TEHN**
the **pie**	el pastel	ehl **pahss-TEHL**
the **plates**	los platos	lohss **PLAH-tohss**
the **sandwich**	el sándwich	el **SAHND-weech**
the **water**	el agua	ehl **AH-gwah**
this	esta	**EHSS-tah**

PEEL _____ (THE POTATOES)
Pele _____ (las papas)
PEH-leh _____ (lahss PAH-pahss)

COMMON CHOICES

the **apples**	las manzanas	lahss **mahn-ZAH-nahss**
the **carrots**	las zanahorias	lahss **sahn-ah-OH-ree-ahss**
the **cucumbers**	los pepinos	lohss **peh-PEE-nohss**
the **onions**	las cebollas	lahss **seh-BOH-yahss**
the **potatoes**	las papas	lahss **PAH-pas**
the **eggplants**	las berenjenas	lahss **beh-rehn-HEH-nahss**
these	estos	**EHSS-tohss**
this	esta	**EHSS-tah**

PUT _____(THE DELIVERY) AWAY.

Pone _____ (la entrega).

POH-neh _____ (lah ehn-TREH-gah).

COMMON CHOICES

the **beer**	la cervesa	lah *sair* -VEH-sah
the **cake**	la torta	lah **TOHR-tah**
the **fish**	el pescado	ehl **pehss-KAH-doh**
the **food**	el comido	ehl **koh-MEE-doh**
the **fruit**	las frutas	lahss **FROO-tahss**
the **glasses**	las vasos	lahss **VAH-sohss**
the **groceries**	los comestibles	lohss **koh-mehss-TEE-blehss**
the **linens**	las ropas blancas	lahss **ROH-pahss BLAHN-kahss**
the **meat**	la carne	lah **KAHR-nay**
the **plates**	los platos	lohss **PLAH-tohss**
the **silverware**	los objetos de plata	lohss **ohb-HEH-tohss deh PLAH-tah**
this	esta	**EHSS-tah**
the **vegetables**	los vegetales	*lohss* **veh-jeh-TAH-lehs**

REPLACE _____ (THE LIGHTBULB)
Reponé _____ (la bombilla) (las bombillas)
reh-poh-NEY _____ (lah bohm-BEE-yah) (lahss bohm-BEE-yahss)

COMMON CHOICES

the **coffee cups**	las tazas para café	lahss **TAH-sahss PAH-rah kah-FAY**
the **doorknob**	el tirador	ehl **tee-RAH-dohr**
the **glasses**	los vasos	lohs **VAH-sohss**
the **handle**	la manija	lah **mahn-EE-hah**
the **linens**	las ropas blancas	lahss **ROH-pahss BLAHN-kahss**
the **paper towels**	las toallas papel lahss	lahss **toh-AH-yah pah-PEL**
the **silverware**	los objetos de plata	lohss **oh-BEH-tohss day plah-tohss**
the **toilet paper**	el papel hygienico	ehl **pah-PEL ee-he-EN-ee-koh**
the **window**	la ventana	la **ven-TAH-nah**
this	esta	**EHSS-tah**

SLICE _____ (THE BACON)
Rebane _____(el tocino)
reh-BAH-neh _____(ehl toh-SEE-noh)

COMMON CHOICES

the **bread**	el pan	ehl **pahn**
the **cake**	la torta	lah **TOHR-tah**
the **carrots**	las zanahorias	lahss **sahn-ah-OH-ree-ahss**
the **cheese**	el queso	ehl **KAY-soh**
the **ham**	el jamon	ehl **hah-MOHN**
the **lemons**	los limónes	lohss **lee-MOHN-ess**
the **limes**	las limas	lahss **LEE-mahss**
the **meat**	el carne	ehl **KAHR-nay**
the **onions**	las cebollas	lahss **seh-BOH-yahss**
the **oranges**	las naranjas	lahss **nah-RAHN-hahss**
the **pie**	el pastel	ehl **pahss-TEHL**
the **watermelon**	la sandía	lah **sahn-DEE-ah**
this	esta	**EHSS-tah**

WASH THE _____(THE DISHES)
Lava _____(los platos)
LAH-vah _____(lohss PLAH-tohss)

COMMON CHOICES

counter	el mostrador	**ehl mohss-trah-DOHR**
floor	el piso	**ehl PEE-soh**
food	el comido	**ehl koh-MEE-doh**
laundry	la lavandaría	**lah lah-bahn-dah-REE-ah**
machines	las maquinas	**lahss mah-KEE-nahss**
ovens	los ornos	**lohss OHR-nohss**
silverware	los objetos de plata	**lohss ohb-heh-tohss day PLAH-tah**
tables	las mesas	**lahss MEH-sahss**
this	este	**EHSS-tay**
vegetables	los vegetales	**lohss veh-jeh-TAH-lays**
wall	el pared	**ehl pah-REHD**
windows	las ventanas	**lahss vehn-TAH-nahss**

COMPLEX SENTENCES
(Go to THE GLOSSARY for other choices)

_____(The waitress) needs _____(clean glasses)
_____(La camarera) necesita _____ (vasos limpios)
_____(lah kahm-ah-REHR-ah) neh-seh-SEE-tah _____(VAH-sohss LEEM-pee-ohss)

Fill _____ (the pot) with _____(water).
Llene _____(la olla) con _____(agua).
YAY-neh _____(lah OH-yah) kohn _____(AH-gwah).

How many _____(eggs) do we have in _____ (the walk-in)?
¿Cuantos _____(huevos) tenemos en _____(el cuarto frío)?
KWAHN-tohss _____(hway -vohss) teh-NEH-mohss ehn _____(el KWAHR-toh FREE-oh)

Put _____ (the tablecloths) _____(on the tables).
Pone _____ (los manteles) _____ (sobre las mesas)
POH-neh __ (lohss mahn-TEH-lehss) _ (SOH-breh lahss MEH-sahss)

Take _____ (this knife) _____ (to the chef)
Lleva _____ (esta cuchillo) _____ (al cocinero).
YAY-vah _____ (ESS-tah koo-CHEE-oh) _____(ahl koh-see NEHR-oh).

Go _____ (downstairs) and get _____(milk)
Vaya _____ (piso bajo) y traiga _____(leche)
BAH-yah _____ (PEE-soh BAH-hoh) EE *TRY*-gah _____ (LEH-cheh)

NUMBERS

one	uno	**OOH-noh**
two	dos	**dohss**
three	tres	**trayss**
four	quatro	**KWHAH-troh**
five	cinco	**SEEN-koh**
six	séis	**SEH-eess**
seven	siete	**see-EHT-tay**
eight	ocho	**OH-choh**
nine	nueve	**NWEH-vay**
ten	diés	**dee-ESS**
eleven	once	**OHN-say**
twelve	doce	**DOH-say**
thirteen	trece	**TREH-say**
fourteen	catorce	**kah-TOHR-say**
fifteen	quince	**KEEN-say**

sixteen	diez y seis	**dee-EHSS ee SAY-ees**
seventeen	diez y siete	**dee-EHSS ee see-EHT-tay**
eighteen	diez y ocho	**dee-EHSS ee OH-cho**
nineteen	dies y nueve	**dee-EHSS ee NWAY-vay**
twenty	veinte	**BEHN-tay**
thirty	treinta	**TREHN-tah**
forty	cuarenta	**qwah-REHN-tah**
fifty	cincuenta	**seen-QWHEN-tah**
sixty	sesenta	**seh-SEN-tah**
seventy	setenta	**seh-TEN-tah**
eighty	ochenta	**oh-CHEN-tah**
ninety	noventa	**no-VEN-tah**
one hundred	ciento	**see-EHN-toh**
two hundred	doscientos	**doh-see-EHN-tohss**
three hundred	trescientos	**trehs-ee-EHN-tohss**
four hundred	cuatrosientos	**qwa-troh-see-EHN-tohss**
five hundred	quinientos	**keen-ee-EHN-tohss**
six hundred	seiscientos	**seh-ee-see-EHN-tohss**

seven hundred	setecientos	**seh-teh-see-EHN-tohss**
eight hundred	ochocientos	**oh-choh-see-EHN-tohss**
nine hundred	novecientos	**noh-veh-see-EHN-tohss**
one thousand	un mil	**oon meel**

first	primero	**pree-MEH-rroh**
second	segundo	**seh-GOON-doh**
third	tercero	**tehr-SEH-rroh**
fourth	cuarto	**KWAHR-toh**
fifth	quinto	**KEEN-toh**
sixth	sexto	**SEHX-toh**
seventh	séptimo	**SEHP-tee-moh**
eighth	octavo	**ohk-TAH-boh**
ninth	noveno	**noh-BAY-noh**
tenth	décimo	**DEH-see-moh**
next	próximo	**PRROHX-ee-moh**
last	último	**OOL-tee-moh**

WEIGHTS AND MEASURES

inch	pulgada	**pool-GAH-dah**
foot	pie	**PEE-aa**
yard	yarda	**YAHR-dah**
mile	milla	**MEE-lyah**
teaspoon	cucharilla	**koo-cha-REE-ah**
tablespoon	cuchara	**koo-CHAH-rah**
ounce	onza	**OHN-sah**
half-pint	media pinta	**MAY-dee-ah PEEN-tah**
pint	pinta	**PEEN-tah**
quart	cuarta de galón	**KWAHR-tah day gah-LOHN**
gallon	galón	**gah-LOHN**

DAYS OF THE WEEK

Sunday	domingo	**doh-MEEN-goh**
Monday	lunes	**LOO-nehs**
Tuesday	martes	**MAHR-tehs**
Wednesday	miércoles	**mee-EHR-koh-lehs**
Thursday	jueves	**HWAY-vehs**
Friday	viernes	**vee-EHR-nehs**
Saturday	sábado	**SAH-bah-doh**
Daily	diariamente	**dee-ah-ree-ah-MEHN-tay**
From now on	desde ahora	**DEHS-deh ah-ORR-ah**
In the afternoon	en la tarde	**ehn lah TAHR-day**
In the morning	en la mañana	**ehn lah mahn-YAH-nah**
In the night	En la noche	**ehn lah NOH-chay**
Last night	anoche	**ah-NOH-chay**

Last week	Semana pasada	seh-MAHN-ah pah-SAH-dah
last year	antaño	ahn-TAHN-yoh
Later	Más tarde	MAHSS TAHR-day
Never	Nunca	NOON-kah
Next week	Próxima semana	PROHX-ee-mah seh-MAHN-ah
Next year	Próximo año	PROHX-ee-moh AHN-yoh
Right now	ahora mismo	ah-ORR-ah MEESS-moh
This afternoon	esta tarde	EHSS-tah TAHR-day
This evening	esta noche	EHSS-tah NOH-chay
This morning	esta mañana	EHSS-tah mahn-YAH-nah
Today	hoy	oy
Tomorrow	mañana	mahn-YAH-nah
Yesterday	ayer	ah-YEHR

MONTHS OF THE YEAR

January	enero	**eh-NAIR -oh**
February	febrero	**feh-BREH-roh**
March	marzo	**MAHR-soh**
April	abríl	**ah-BREEL**
May	mayo	**MAH-yoh**
June	junio	**HOO-nyoh**
July	julio	**HOO-lee-yoh**
August	agosto	**ah-GOHSS-toh**
September	septiembre	**sehp-tee-EM-bray**
October	octubre	**ohk-TOO-bray**
November	noviembre	**noh-vee-EHM-bray**
December	diciembre	**dee-see-EHM-bray**

TIMES OF THE DAY

(At) One o'clock	(A) la una	(ah) lah OO-nah
(At) One fifteen	(A) la una y quince	(ah) lah OO-nah ee keen-say
(At) One thirty	(A) la una y média	(ah) lah OO-nah ee MEH-dee-ah
(At) One forty five	(A) la una y cuarenta y cinco	(ah) la OO-nah ee qwah-REHN-tah ee SEEN-koh
(At) A quarter to two	(A) las dos menos cuarto	(ah) lahss dohss MEH-nohss QWAHR-toh
(At) Two o'clock	(A) las dos	(ah) lahss dohss
(At) Three o'clock	(A) las tres	(ah) lahss trehss
(At) Four o'clock	(A) las cuatro	(ah) lahss QWAH-trroh
(At) Five o'clock	(A) las cinco	(ah) lahss SEEN-koh
(At) Six o'clock	(A) las seis	(ah) lahss SEH-eess
(At) Seven o'clock	(A) las siete	(ah) lahss see-EHT-tay
(At) Eight o'clock	(A) las ocho	(ah) lahss OH-choh
(At) Nine o'clock	(A) las nueve	(ah) lahss NWAY-vay
(At) Ten o'clock	(A) las diez	(ah) lahss dee-ESS
(At) Eleven o'clock	(A) las once	(ah) lahss OHN-say

(At) Twelve o'clock	(A) las doce	**(ah) lahss DOH-say**
Noon	Mediodía	**meh-dee-oh-DEE-ah**
Midnight	Media noche	**MEH-dee-ah NOH-chay**
In the afternoon	en la tarde	**ehn lah TAHR-day**
In the morning	en la mañana	**ehn lah mahn-YAH-nah**
in the night	en la noche	**ehn lah NOH-chay**

COLORS

Black	negro	**NEH-groh**
White	blanco	**BLAHN-koh**
Red	rojo	**RROH-hoh**
Green	verde	**V*AIR*-deh**
Yellow	amarillo	**ah-mah-REE-yoh**
Blue	azul	**ah-SOOL**
Gold	oro	**OAR-oh**
Silver	plata	**PLAH-tah**
Orange	naranja	**nah-RAHN-ha**

Brown	moreno	**moh-RAY-noh**
Gray	gris	**GREESS**
Pink	rosa	**RROH-sah**

PERSONNEL

The boss	(el) jefe	ehl **HEH-feh**
The chef /cook	(el) cocinero	ehl **koh-see-NEHR-oh**
The waitress	(la) camarera	lah **kah-mah-REH-rah**
The waiter	(el) camarero	ehl **kah-mah-REH-roh**
The bartender	(el) mozo de taberna	ehl **MOH-ssoh deh-tah-BEHR-nah**
The dishwasher	(el) lavaplato	ehl **lah-vah-PLAH-tohh**
The busboy	(el) ayudante de camarero	**ah-yoo-DAHN-tay day cah-mah-REH-roh**
The cashier	(el) cajero	ehl **kah-HEHR-OH**
The valet	(el) criado	ehl **kree-AH-doh**
The doorman	(el) portero	ehl **poh-TEHR-oh**

THE INTERVIEW

Hello!	¡Hola!	OH-lah
Sit down please.	Por favor siéntese.	pohr fah-VOHR see-EHN-teh-say
My Name is . . .	Me llamo...	may YAH-moh...
What is your name?	¿Como se llama?	KOH-moh say YAH-mah
Do you speak English?	¿Habla Inglés?	AH-blahss eeng-GLEHSS
Do you have any references?	¿Tienes referencias?	tee-EH-nehss reh-feh-REHN-see-ahss
Do you live nearby?	¿Tu vives cerca de aquí?	too BEE-bess SEHR-kah deh ah-KEE
Is it a problem to travel here?	¿Le es dificil venir aquí	lay ehss dee-FEE-seel behn-EER ah-KEE
Are you an American citizen?	¿Tu eres ciudadano Americano?	
	too EHR-ehss see-yu-dah-DAH-no ah-meh-ree-KAH-noh	
Do you have a green card?	¿Tiene tarjeta de residente?	
	tee-EH-neh tahr-HEH-tah deh reh-see-DEHN-tay	
Do you have a drivers license?	¿Tiene licencia para manajar?	
	tee-EH-nay lee-SEN-see ah PAH-rah mahn-ah-HAHR	

Do you have experience ?
¿Tiene experiencia?
tee-EH-nay ex-peh-ree-EHN-see ah

Can you work overtime when necessary?
¿Puede trabajar horas extras cuando se necesita?
PWEH-day trah-bah-HARR OHR-ahss ES-trahss KWAN-doh neh-seh-SEE-tah

Can you work (nights)(weekends)?
¿Puede trabajar en (las noches)(los fines de semana)
PWEH-deh trah-bah-HARR ehn (lahss NOH-chess)(lohss FEE-nehss deh seh-MAH-nah)

The pay is $ _____per hour.
El pago es $ _____por hora.
ell PAH-goh ess _____ pohr OH-rah

Please fill this out.
Por favor, completa este.
pohr fah-VOHR kohm-PLEH-tah es-tay

Please print.
Por favór, escriba en letra de molde.
pohr fah-VOHR, eh-SKREE-bah ehn LEH-trah day MOHL-day.

What is your telephone number?
¿Que es el número de su teléfono?
kay ess ell NOO-meh-roh day soo teh-LEH-foh-noh

THE GLOSSARY

adhesive tape	tela adhesiva	TEH-lah ahd-hehs-EE-vah
adult	adulto	ah-DOOL-toh
air conditioner	aire conditionado	I-ray kohn-dee-see-oh-NAH-doh
air filter	filtro de aire	FEEL-troh day I-ray
airplane	aeroplano	*air* -oh-PLAH-noh
alarm clock	despertador	dess-pehr-TAH-dor
alcohol	alcohol	ahl-KOH-hohl
ale	cervesa inglesa muy fuerte	sehr-VEH-sah een-GLESS-ah mwee F*WHERE* -tay
alley	pasadizo	pah-sah-DEE-zoh
almond	almendra	ahl-MEN-drah
aluminum foil	papel de aluminio	pah-PELL day ah-loo-MEE-nyoh
American cheese	queso Americano	KAY-soh ah-meh-ree-KAH-noh
ammonia	amonia	ah-moh-NEE-yah
amplifier	amplificador	ahm-plee-fee-KAH-dohr
anchovies	anchoas	ahn-CHOH-ahss
anise	anís	ahn-EESS

antidote	contraveneno	**kohn-trah-veh-NEH-noh**
appetizer	aperitivo	**ah-pehr-eh-TEE-voh**
apple	manzana	**mahn-ZAH-nah**
apple sauce	salsa de manzana	**SAHL-sah day mahn-SSAH-nah**
apricot	albaricoque	**ahl-bah-ree-KOH-keh**
April	abril	**ah-BREEL**
apron	delantal	**deh-lahn-TAHL**
arm	brazo	**BRAH-soh**
artichoke	alcachofa	**ahl-kah-CHOH-fah**
artificial flower	flores artificiales	**FLOHR-ess ahr-tee-fee-see-AHL-ess**
ashtrays	cenizeros	**sehn-ee-SEHR-ohss**
asparagus	espárrago	**ess-PAH-rah-goh**
assistant	ayudante	**ah-yoo-DAHN-tay**
asst. manager	asistente al gerente	**ah-sees-TEN-tay ahl-geh-REHN-teh**
aunt	tía	**TEE-ah**
avocado	aguacate	**ah-gwah-KAH-tay**
axe	segur	**say-GOOR**
baby chair	silla para el niño	**SEE-yah PAH-rah NEE-nyoh**

baby	pequeño	peh-KANE-yoh
back door	puerta trasero	*PWHERE*-tah trah-SEH-roh
bacon	tocino	toh-SEE-noh
bag	saco	SAH-coh
baked potato	papa horno	PAH-pah OHR-noh
bakery	panadería	pahn-ah-deh-REE-ah
baking powder	polvo para hornada	POHL-voh PAH-rah ohr-NAH-dah
baking soda	soda para hornada	SOH-dah PAH-rah ohr NAH-dah
banana	banana	bah-NAH-nah
band	banda	BAHN-dah
band stand	tarima de banda	tah-REE-mah deh BAHN-dah
bandage	venda	BEHN-dah
banquet	banquete	bahn-KEH-tay
banquet hall	salón de banquete	sah-LOHN deh bahn-KEH-tay
bar	barra	BAHR-rah
bar napkins	servilletas para la barra	sehr-vee-EH-tahss PAH-rah lah BAH-rrah
barbeque	barbacoa	bahr-bah-KOH-ah
barbequed meat	churrasco	chew-RRAHSS-koh

barbeque sauce	salsa de babacoa	SAHL-sah deh bahr-bah-KOH-ah
barley	cebada	seh-BAH-dah
bartender	mozo de taberna	MOH-ssoh day tah-BEHR-nah
basil	basíl	bah-SEEL
basket	capacho	kah-PAH-choh
bathrooms	los baños	lohss BAHN-yohss
bathroom sink	lavabo	lah-VAH-boh
bay leaf	laurel	lah-oo-REHL
beans	frijoles	free-HOH-lehss
beans(kidney)	habichuelas	ha-bee-CH*WAY*-lahss
bean curd	cuajada de haba	kwah-HAH-dah day AH-bah
bean sprouts	retoño de haba	reh-TOHN-yoh day AH-bah
because	porqué	pohr-KAY
beef	carne de vaca	KAHR-nay day BAH-kah
beer	cerveza	sehr-VEH-sah
beer glasses	vasos de cervesa	VAH-sohss deh sehr-VEH-sah
beer kegs	barril de cervesa	bar-RREEL deh sehr-VEH-sah
beets	remolachas	ray-moh-LAH-chahss

bellboy	mozo del hotel	**MOH-soh del OH-tel**
belt	cinturo	**seen-TOO-roh**
beverage	bebida	**bay-BEE-dah**
bill (the)	la cuenta	**lah Q*WHEN*-tah**
bird (fowl)	ave	**AH-vay**
biscuit	bizcocho	**beess-KOH-choh**
bitter	amargo	**ah-MAR-goh**
black olives	olivas negras	**oh-LEE-vahss NEH-grahss**
black pepper	pimienta	**pee-mee-EN-tah**
blackberry	zarzamora	**sahr-sah-MOH-rah**
blackfish	pescado negro	**pehss-KAH-doh NEH-groh**
black sea bass	róbalo negro	**ROH-bah-loh NEH-groh**
bleach	blancque	**BLAHN-kay**
blender	licuadora	**lee-kwah-DOHR-ah**
blood	sangre	**SAHN-gray**
blue	azul	**AH-ssool**
blue cheese	queso azul	**KAY-soh ah-SOOL**
blueberries	bayas azules	**BAH-yahss ah-SOOL-ehss**

boiled	salcochado	sahl-koh CHAH-doh
boiling	hervidero	*air*-vee-DARE-oh
bologna	mortadela	mor-tah-DEHL-ah
bones	huesos	WAY-sohss
boning knives	cuchillo pequeño	koo-CHEE-yoh peh-KAY-nyoh
book	libro	LEE-broh
booth	casilla	kah-SEE-yah
boss	jefe	HEH-fay
bosses wife	esposa del patrón	ess-POH-sah del pah-TRROHN
bottle	botella	boh-TEH-yah
bouquet	ramillete	rah-mee-YAY-tay
bowl	escudilla	ess-koo-DEE-yah
brains	sesos	SEH-sohss
brandy	coñac	KOH-nyak
brass railing	riel latón	REE-ehl lah-TOHN
Brazil nuts	nuez de Brazil	new-EHZ deh brrah-SEEL
bread (rye)	pan de centeno	pahn day sehn-TEHN-oh
bread (white)	pan blanco	pahn BLAHN-koh

bread basket	cesto para el pan	**SEHS-toh PAH-rah ehl pahn**
bread crumbs	arina del pan	**ah-REE nah dehl pahn**
bread knives	cuchillos para pan	**koo-CHEE-yohss PAH-rah pahn**
bread	pan	**pahn**
bread plates	platos para pan	**PLAH-tohss PAH-rah pahn**
breakfast	desayuno	**deh-seh-OO-noh**
brillo	brillo	**BRREE-yoh**
broccoli	bróculi	**BRROH-koo-lee**
broken	quebrado	**kay-BRAH-doh**
broom	escoba	**ess-KOH-bah**
brother	hermano	**ehr-MAHN-oh**
brown	moreno	**mohr-EH-noh**
brown sugar	azucar morena	**ah-SOO-kahr mohr-EH-nah**
brush	cepillo	**seh-PEE-yoh**
brussel sprouts	coles de Bruselas	**KOH-lehss deh broo-SEH-lahss**
bucket	cubo	**KOO-boh**
bulb	bombilla	**bohm-BEE-yah**
burners	mecheros	**meh-CHEHR-ohss**

busboy	ayudante de camarero	ah-yoo-DAHN-teh day cah-mah-*RAIR*-oh
buscuit	galleta	gah-YEH-tah
butcher's paper	papel para el carnicero	pah-PELL PAH-rah ehl kahr-nee-SEH-roh
butcher's table	mesa para el carnicero	MEH-sah PAH-rah ehl kahr-nee-SEH-roh
butter chips	pedacito de mantequilla	peh-dah-SEE-toh day mahn-teh-KEE-yah
butter dishes	platos para mantequilla	PLAH-tohss PAH-rah mahn-teh-KEE-yah
butter knives	cuchillos de mantequilla	koo-CHEE-yohss day mahn-teh-KEE-yah
butter	mantequilla	mahn-teh-KEE-yah
cabana	cabaña	kah-BAHN-yah
cabbage	repollo	ray-POH-yoh
cabbage(red)	repollo rojo	reh-POH-yoh ROH-hoh
cafeteria	restaurante	rehs-tahr-AHN-tay
cake	torta	TOHR-tah
calculator	máquina calculadora	MAH-kee-nah kahl-koo-lah-DOHR-ah
calendar	calandario	kah-lahn-DAH-ree-oh
can opener	abrelata	ah-breh-LAH-tah
candle holders	candeleros	kahn-deh-LEHR-rohss
candles	candelas	kahn-DEH-lahss

candy	confitura	**kohn-fee-TOO-rah**
canned	en lata	**ehn LAH-tah**
cantaloupe	melón	**meh-LOHN**
capers	alcaparras	**ahl-kah-PAHR-rass**
car	carro	**KAH-rroh**
carafe	garrafa	**hah-RRAH-fah**
carp	carpa	**KAR-pah**
carpenter	carpintero	**kahr-peen-TEHR-oh**
carrot	zanahoria	**sahn-ah-OH-ree-ah**
case	caja	**KAH-hah**
cashier	cajero	**kah-HEHR-oh**
cash register	caja registradora	**KAH-hah reh-HEESS-trah-dohr-ah**
casino	casino	**kah-SEE-noh**
cauliflower	coliflor	**koh-LEE-flohr**
caviar	caviar	**kah-VEE-ahr**
ceiling(s)	techo(s)	**TEH-choh(ss)**
celery	apio	**ah-PEE-oh**
centerpiece	ramillete	**rah-mee-YAY-tay**

cereal	cereal	seh-REH-ahl
chair of honor	sitial	SEE-tee-ahl
chair	silla	SEE-ya
champagne	champaña	shahm-PAHN-yah
champagne glasses	vasos para champaña	BAH-sohss PAH-rah shahm-PAHN-yah
champagne vinegar	champaña de vinagre	shahm-PAHN-yah day vee-NAH-greh
cheese(American)	queso Americano	KAY-soh ah-meh-ree-KAH-noh
chef	cocinero	koh-see-NEHR-oh
chef's knives	cuchillos de cocinero	koo-CHEE-yohss day koh-see-NEHR-oh
cherries	cerezas	seh-REH-sahss
chestnuts	castañas	kah-STAHN-yahss
chick pea	garbanzo	gahr-BAHN-soh
chicken (roast)	pollo asado	POH-yoh ah-SAH-doh
chicken breasts	pechuga de pollo	peh-CHEW-gah day POH-yoh
chicken cutlets	chuletas de pollo	choo-LEH-tahss day POH-yoh
chicken	pollo	POH-yoh
chicken fat	grasa del pollo	GRAH-sah dehl POH-yoh
chicken soup	sopa de pollo	SOH-pah deh POH-yoh

chicken(whole)	pollo entero	POH-yoh ehn-TEHR-oh
chicory	achicoria	ah-chee-koh-REE-yah
child	niño(a)	NEE-nyoh (nyah)
chili pepper	ají	ah-HEE
chili powder	polvo de chili	POHL-voh day CHEE-lee
chili sauce	salsa de chili	SAHL-sah day CHEE-lee
chives	ceballitos	seh-bah-YEE-tohss
chocolate	chocolate	choh-koh-LAH-tay
chop (of meat)	chuleta	chew-LEH-tah
cider	sidra	SEE-drah
cigar	cigarro	see-GAH-rroh
cigarette	cigarillo	see-gah-EE-yoh
cinnamon	canela	kah-NEH-lah
clams	almejas	ahl-MAY-hahss
claret	clarete	klah-REH-tay
cleaver	hacha	AH-chah
clothes dryer	secadora de ropa	seh-kah-DOHR-ah day ROH-pah
clothing	ropa	ROH-pah

cloves(whole)	diente	dee-EHN-tay
coat check attendant	guardadór de chaqueta	gwhar-dah-DOHR day chah-KEH-tah
cockaroach	cucaracha	koo-kah-RAH-chah
cocktail forks	tenedoras pequeños	teh-neh-DOHR-ahss peh-KEHN-yohss
cocoa	cacao	kah-KOW
coconut	coco	KOH-koh
cod	bacalao	bah-kahl-OW
coffee (instant)	café instantanio	kah-FAY een-stahn-TAH-nee-oh
coffee	café	kah-FAY
coffee cup	taza para café	TAH-sah PAH-rah kah-FAY
coffee filters	filtros de café	FEEL-trohss day kah-FAY
coffee machine	maquina de café	mah-KEE-nah day kah-FAY
coffee pot	cafetera	kah-feh-TEH-rah
coffee urn	cafeteria	kah-feh-TEH-ree-ah
colander	colador	koh-lah-DOHR
cold drink	refresco	reh-FRES-koh
cold	frío	FREE-oh
cold meal	comida fria	koh-MEE-dah FREE-ah

complaint	quejido	keh-HEE-doh
compote	compota	kohm-POH-tah
container	recipiente	reh-see-pee-EHN-tay
cook	cocinero	koh-see-NEHR-oh
cooked	cocido	koh-SEE-doh
cooking	cocinando	koh-see-NAHN-doh
corkscrew	tira buzón	TEER-ah boo-ZOHN
corn	maíz	mah-EESS
corn starch	almidon	ahl-MEE-dohn
corn syrup	jarabe de maíz	hah-RAH-bay day mah-EESS
corned beef	vaca en conserva	VAH-kah ehn kohn-SEHR-vah
cost	coste	KOH-stay
counter	mostrador	mohss-trah DOHR
cousin	primo (prima)	PREE-moh (mah)
crab	cangrejo	kahn-GREH-hoh
crackers	galletas	gahl-YEH-tass
cranberry	arándano	ah-RRAHN-dah-noh
cranberry sauce	salsa de arándano	SAHL-sah day ah-RRAHN-dah-noh

cream	crema	KREH-mah
cream (heavy)	crema espesa	KREH-mah ess-PEH-sah
cream (whipped)	crema batida	KREH-mah bah-TEE-dah
creamers	jarros para crema	HAH-rohss PAH-rah KREH-mah
creole	criollo	kree-OH-yoh
cruet stand	vinagreras	been-ah-GREHR-ahss
cruets	ampollas	ahm-POH-yahss
crust	corteza	kohr-TEH-ssah
cucumber	pepino	peh-PEE-noh
cumin	comino	koh-MEE-noh
cup	taza	TAH-ssah
cup (teacup)	taza para té	TAH-sah PAH-rah tay
cup (coffee cup)	taza para café	TAH-sah PAH-rah kah-FAY
cup of tea	taza de té	TAH-sah day tay
curry	condimento de origen indio	kohn-dee-MEN-toh deh oh-REE-hen EEN-dee-oh
curtains	cortinas	kohr-TEE-nahs
custard	natillas	nah-TEE-yahs
customer	cliente	klee-EHN-tay

cutlery	cubiertos	koo-bee-EHR-tohss
cutlet	chuleta	chew-LEH-tah
damp	húmedo	OO-meh-doh
dance floor	suelo de baile	SWEH-loh deh BY-lay
dandelion greens	diente de león	dee-EHN-tay day ley-OHN
dangerous	peligroso	peh-lee-GROH-soh
date (fruit)	dátil	DAH-teel
daughter	hija	EE-hah
day	día	DEE-ah
day off	día libre	DEE-ah LEE-bray
dáis	estrado	ess-TRAH-doh
de-odorizer	desodorante	deh-ssoh-dohr-AHN-tay
December	diciembre	dee-cee-EM-bray
deep-fryer	máquina para freidura	MAH-kee-nah PAH-rah freh-ee-DOO-rah
delivery	entrega	ehn-TREH-gah
desk	pupitre	poo-PEE-tray
dessert	postre	POH-stray
detergent	detergente	deh-tehr-HEHN-tay

dice	dados	DAH-dohss
dill	eneldo	eh-NEHL-doh
dining room	comedor	koh-meh-DOHR
dinner plates	platos de cema	PLAH-tohss day SEH-mah
dinner time	hora de comer	OHR-ah day koh-MEHR
dirt	suciedad	soo-see-aa-DAHD
dirty	sucio	SOO-see-oh
dish (bowl)	fuente	FWHEN-tay
dish racks	escurreplatos	ess-koo-reh-PLAH-tohss
dish soap	jabón de platos	hah-BOHN day PLAH-tohss
dishwasher	lavaplato	lah-vah-PLAH-tohh
disinfectant	disinfectante	deess-een-fehk-TAHN-tay
door knob	tirador	tee-RAH-dohr
door	puerta	PWHERE-tah
doorman	portero	poh-TEHR-oh
doughnut	buñuelo	boo-NWEH-loh
downstairs	piso bajo	PEE-soh BAH-hoh
drain cleaner	detergente para el drenaje	deh-tehr-HEHN-teh PAH-rah ehl dreh-NAH-heh

drugs	drogas	**DROH-gahss**
drunk	borracho	**boh-RRAH-choh**
dry	seco	**SEH-koh**
duck	pato	**PAH-toh**
duckling	patico	**pah-TEE-koh**
early	temprano	**tehm-PRAH-noh**
earthquake	seísmo	**say-EES-moh**
eel	anguila	**ahn-GEE-lah**
egg white	clara	**KLAH-rah**
egg yolk	yema	**YEH-mah**
eggplant	berenjena	**beh-rehn-HEH-nah**
eggs	huevos	**H*WAY*-vohss**
electric plug	enchufe	**ehn-*CHEW*-fay**
electrical outlet	enchuflé electrico	**en-*chew*-FLAY ee-LEHK-tree-koh**
electrical wire	alambre para la electricidad	**ah-LAHM-bray PAH-rah lah eh-lehk-TRIH-see-dahd**
electrician	electricista	**ee-lehk-tree-SEE-stah**
electricity	electricidad	**eh-lehk-trih-see-DAHD**
elevator	ascensor	**ahs-SEHN-sohr**

emergency exit	salida de emergencio	**sah-LEE-dah deh eh-mehr HEN-syoh**
emergency lights	luces de emergencio	**LOO-sehss deh eh-mehr HEN-syoh**
employee	empleado	**ehm-pleh-AH-doh**
employees' lounge	cuarto para lecansar	**KWAHR-toh PAH-rah leh-KAHN-sahr**
employer	patrón	**pah-TROHN**
empty	vacío	**vah-SEE-oh**
endive	escarola	**ess-kah-ROH-lah**
entrance	entrada	**ehn-TRAH-dah**
entreé	principio	**preen-SEE-pee-o**
everyday	cotidiaro	**koo-tee-dee-AH-roh**
excuse	excusa	**es-KOO-sah**
exit	salida	**sah-LEE-dah**
extention cord	cordón de extención	**kohr-DOHN deh ex-tehn-see-OHN**
exterminator	extinctor	**es-TEENK-tohr**
extra pay	sobresueldo	**so-breh-SWEHL-doh**
fat (grease)	grasa	**GRAH-sah**
father	padre	**PAH-dray**
faucets	grifos	**GREE-fohss**

fig	higo	EE-goh
filled	relleño	reh-YEH-nyoh
fillet	filete	fee-LEH-tay
finger	dedo del mano	DEH-doh del MAHN-oh
fire extinguisher	extintor	es-TEEN-tohr
fire	fuego	FWEH-goh
first aid kit	botiquín	boh-tee-KEEN
fish	pescado	pehs-KAH-doh
flashlight	linterna eléctrica	leen-TEHR-nah ee-LEHK-tree-kah
floor mats	estera para el piso	ehs-TEH-rah PAH-rah el PEE-soh
floor(s)	piso(s)	PEE-soh(ss)
flour	harina	ah-REE-nah
flounder	platija	plah-TEE-hah
flower pot	tiesto	tee-ESS-toh
flowers	floras	FLOH-rahss
fluorescent bulb	luz florescente	loose flohr-ess-SEHN-teh
fly	mosca	MOH-skah
food	comida	koh-MEE-dah

foot	pie	**PEE-ay**
forks	tenedoras	**teh-neh-DOHR-ahss**
freezer	congelador	**kohn-heh-lah-DOHR**
French fries	papas fritas	**PAH-pas FREE-tas**
fresh	fresco	**FREHSS-coh**
fried	frito	**FREE-toh**
frog's legs	patas de rana	**PAH-tahss day RAH-nah**
from now on	desde ahora	**DES-day ah-OHR-ah**
front entrance	entrada delantero	**ehn-TRAH-dah deh-lahn-TEHR-oh**
frozen	helado	**eh-LAH-doh**
fruit	fruta	**FROO-tah**
frying pan	sartén	**sahr-TEHN**
full	repleto	**ray-PLEH-toh**
funeral	entierro	**en-TYEH-rroh**
funnel	embudo	**em-BOO-doh**
furnace	horno	**OHR-noh**
fuses	fusibles	**foo-SEE-blehs**
gallon	galón	**gah-LOHN**

garbage	basura	**bah-SOO-rah**
garbage bag	saco para basura	**SAH-koh PAH-rah bah-SOO-rah**
garbage pail	cesto	**SEHSS-toh**
garlic	ajo	**AH-hoh**
gas	gas	**gahss**
gate	puerto	**P*WHERE*-toh**
gauze	gasa	**GAH-sah**
gelatin	gelatina	**hell-ah-TEE-nah**
giblets	menudillos	**mehn-oo-DEE-yohss**
gin	ginebra	**heen-AY-brah**
ginger	jengibre	**hen-HEE-bray**
gingerbread	pan pepato	**pahn peh-PAH-toh**
glass (wine)	copa	**KOH-pah**
glass pitcher	jarra cristál	**HAH-rah kreess-TAHL**
glass racks	estante para vasos	**ess-TAHN-teh PAH-rah VAH-sohss**
glass (window)	cristál	**kreess-TAHL**
glasses	vasos	**VAH-sohss**
gloves	guantes	**GWAHN-tehs**

goose	ganso	**GAHN-soh**
graduation	graduación	**grah-doo-ah-see-OHN**
grandfather	abuelo	**ah-BWEH-loh**
grandmother	abuela	**ah-BWEH-lah**
grape	uva	**OO-bah**
grapefruit	toronja	**toh-ROHN-yah**
grape leaf	hoja de uva	**OH-hah day OO-vah**
gravy	salsa	**SAHL-sah**
gray	gris	**grees**
grease	grasa	**GRAH-sah**
griddle	tartera	**tarh-TEHR-ah**
grille brush	brocha para la parilla	**BROH-chah PAH-rah lah pah-REE-yah**
grille	parilla	**pah-REE-yah**
groceries	comestibles	**koh-mehs-TEE-blehss**
guava	guayaba	**gwah-YAH-bah**
guest	invitado	**in-bee-TAH-doh**
haddock	róbalo	**ROH-bah-loh**
half	medio	**MEH-dee-oh**

English	Spanish	Pronunciation
half pound	media libra	**MEH-dee-ah LEE-brah**
halibut	hipogloso	**ee-poh-GLOH-soh**
hallway	corredor	**kohr-reh-DOHR**
ham	jamon	**hah-MOHN**
hammer	martillo	**mahr-TEE-yoh**
hamper	capacho	**kah-PAH-choh**
hand	mano	**MAH-noh**
handle	manija	**mahn-EE-hah**
hand soap	jabón de mano	**hah-BOHN deh MAH-noh**
handicapped	inválido	**een-VAHL-ee-doh**
hangers	ganchos	**GAHN-chohss**
hare	liebre	**lee-EH-bray**
hash	picadillo	**pee-kah-DEE-yoh**
hat	sombrero	**sohm-BREH-roh**
hazelnuts	avellanas	**ah-vay-YAH-nahs**
head	cabeza	**kah-BEH-sah**
health club	gimnasio	**heem-NAHSS-ee-oh**
health	salud	**sah-LOOD**

GLOSSARY

heat lamp	lámpara calor	**LAHM-pah-rah kah-LOHR**
heavy	pasado	**pah-SAH-doh**
help	ayuda	**ah-YOO-dah**
herb	yerba	**YEHR-bah**
herring	arenque	**ah-REN-kay**
honey	miel	**mee-EL**
hors d' oeurves	entremés	**ehn-treh-MEHSS**
horseradish	rábano picante	**RAH-bah-noh pee-KAHN-tay**
hose	manguera	**mahn-GEHR-rah**
hospital	hospital	**oh-spee-TAHL**
host	hotelero	**oh-tehl-EHR-oh**
hostess	huéspeda	**WAY -speh-dah**
hot & spicy	picante	**pih-KAHN-tay**
hot	caliente	**kah-lee-EHN-tay**
hot lunch	comida caliente	**koh-MEE-dah kahl-ee-EN-tay**
hot water heater	calentador de agua	**kah-lehn-tah-DOHR deh AH-gwah**
hotel	hotel	**oh-TEHL**
hotel keeper	hotelero	**oh-teh-LEHR-oh**

hotel pans	bandejas	bahn-DEH-hahss
housekeeper	casera	kah-SEHR-ah
ice box	nivera	nee-BEHR-ah
ice cream	helado	eh-LAH-doh
ice cream scoop	cucharón para helado	koo-chah-ROHN PAH-rah eh-LAH-doh
ice	hielo	ee-EH-loh
ice cubes	cubitos de hielo	koo-BEE-tohss deh ee-EH-loh
ice machine	máquina de hielo	MAH-kee-nah deh ee-EH-loh
ice scoop	cucharón para hielo	koo-chah-ROHN PAH-rah ee-EH-loh
ice-cream freezer	congelador para helado	kohn-heh-lah-DOHR PAR-rah eh-LAH-doh
icing (sugar)	alcorza	ahl-KOHR-sah
inch	pulgada	pool-GAH-dah
inside	adentro	ah-DEHN-troh
instant potatoes	papas intantañia	PAH-pahss een-stahn-TAHN-ee-yah
intoxicated	embriagado	em-bree-ah-GAH-doh
iodine	yodo	YOH-doh
jacket	chaqueta	chah-KAY-tah
jam	mermelada	mehr-meh-LAH-dah

January	enero	**ehn-EHR-oh**
jelly	jalea	**ha-LEH-ah**
jug	jarro	**HARR-roh**
juice	jugo (de)	**HOO-goh**
juicer	máquina de jugo	**MAH-kee-nah deh HOO-goh**
juicy	zumoso	**soo-MOH-soh**
kettle	caldera	**kahl-DEH-rah**
kidney beans	habichuelas	**ha-bee-CHWEH-lahss**
kidneys	riñones	**ree-NYOH-nehss**
kitchen	cocina	**koh-SEE-nah**
knife (large)	cuchilla	**koo-CHEE-yah**
knife	cuchillo	**koo-CHEE-yoh**
knives (steak)	cuchillos para tajada	**koo-CHEE-yohss PAH-rah tah-HAH-dah**
ladder	escalera	**ess-kah-LEHR-ah**
ladle	cucharón	**koo-chah-ROHN**
lamb	carne de cordero	**KAHR-nay deh kohr-Deh-roh**
lard	manteca	**mahn-TEH-kah**
large	grande	**GRAHN-day**

last	último	**OOL-tee-moh**
late	tardío	**tarh-DEE-oh**
laundry	lavandaría	**lah-bahn-dah-REE-ah**
laundry bag	funda para la ropa	**FOON-dah PAH-rah lah ROH-pah**
laundry room	lavandaría	**lah-bahn-dah-REE-ah**
laundry soap	jabón para la lavandaría	**hah-BOHN PAH-rah lah-bahn-dah-REE-ah**
left	izquierda	**eess-kee-YEHR-dah**
leg	pierna	**pee-EHR-nah**
legume	legumbre	**leh-GOOM-breh**
lemon juice	jugo de limón	**HOO-goh deh lee-MOHN**
lemon	limón	**lee-MOHN**
lemonade	limonada	**lee-mohn-AH-dah**
lentils	lentejas	**lehn-TEH-hahss**
lettuce	lechuga	**leh-CHEW-gah**
lettuce (romaine)	lechuga romana	**leh-CHEW-gah roh-MAH-nah**
lid	tapa	**TAH-pah**
light bulb	foco	**FOH-koh**
light	luz	*LOOSE*

light fixture	lámpara de luz	LAHM-pah-rah day loose
lightswitch	conmutador	kohn-mew-tah-DOHR
lime	lima	LEE-mah
linen	ropa blanca	ROH-pah BLAHN-kah
liquid	líquido	LEE-kee-doh
liquor	licor	lee-KOHR
little	poco	POH-koh
liver	hígado	EE-gah-doh
lobster	langosta	lahn-GOH-stah
lock	cerradura	seh-rah-DOO-rah
locker room	cuarto para cambia ropa	KWAHR-toh PAH-rah KAHM-bee-ah ROH-pah
loin	lomo	LOH-moh
lunch	almuerzo	ahl-M*WHERE*-soh
macaroni	macarrones	mah-kah-RROH-nehss
machine	maquina	MAH-kee-nah
mackerel	caballa	kah-BAH-yah
magazine	revísta	reh-VEESS-tah
malt	malta	MAHL-tah

management	gestoría	hehs-toh-REE-ah
manager	encargado	ehn-kar-GAH-doh
mango	mango	MAHN-goh
maple syrup	jarabe meple	hah-RAH-beh MEH-*play*
market	mercado	mehr-KAH-doh
marmalade	mermelada	mehr-meh-LAH-dah
mashed potatoes	papas molidas	PAH-pahss moh-LEE-dahss
matches	fósforos	FOHSS-foh-rohss
mayonnaise	mayonesa	mah-yoh-NEH-sah
meal	comida	koh-MEE-dah
meal time	hora de comer	OHR-ah deh koh-MEHR
meat (barbequed)	churrasco	chew-RRAHSS-koh
meat (roasted)	carne asado	KAHR-nay ah-SAH-doh
meat	carne	KAHR-nay
meat hammer	martillo para carne	mahr-TEE-yoh PAH-rah KAHR-nay
meat pie	pastel de carne	PAHSS-tel day KAHR-nay
meat (fowl)	carne de pluma	KAR-neh day PLOO-mah
meatballs	albóndigas	ahl-BOHN-dee-gahss

melon	melón	meh-LOHN
menu	menú	meh-NEW
metal pitcher	jarra metal	HAH-rah meh-TAHL
metal plate	plato lata	PLAH-toh LAH-tah
micro-wave	microonda	mee-kroh-OON-dah
microphone	micrófono	mee-KROH-foh-noh
mile	milla	MEE-yah
milk crate	caneca de leche	kah-NEH-kah day LEH-chay
milk	leche	LEH-chay
milkman	lechero	leh-CHEH-roh
mint	hierbabuena	ee-yehr-bah-BWEH-nah
mint jelly	jalea hierbabuena	hah-LEH-ah ee-yehr-bah-BWEH-nah
minute	minuto	mee-NEW-toh
mirror	espejo	ess-PEH-hoh
mixed	mixto	MEE-stoh
mixer	máquina para mezclar	MAH-kee-nah PAH-rah mehss-KLAHR
mixing bowls	taza para mezclar	TAH-sah PAH-rah mehss-KLAHR
Monday	lunes	LOO-ness

month	mez	**MEHSS**
mop bucket	esprimador	**ess-pree-mah-DOHR**
mop	mapo	**MAH-poh**
mother	madre	**MAH-dray**
mouse	ratón	**rah-TOHN**
mouse trap	trampa para los ratónes	**TRAHM-pah PAH-rah lohss rah-TOH-ness**
mushrooms	hongos	**HOHN-gohs**
mussel	caracól	**kah-rah-KOHL**
mustard	mostaza	**moh-STAH-sah**
name	nombre	**NOHM-bray**
napkin (table)	servilleta	**sehr-vee-YEH-tah**
nauseas	tener náuseas	**teh-NEHR NOW-see-ahss**
newspaper	periódico	**peh-ree-OH-dee-koh**
newspaper stand	puesto de periódico	**PWEHS-toh deh peh-ree-OH-dee-koh**
noisy	ruidoso	**rue-ee-DOH-soh**
noodle (thin)	fideo	**fee-DEH-oh**
nut (hazel)	avellana	**ah-veh-YAH-nah**
nutmeg	nuez moscada	*new*-**EZ moh-SKAH-dah**

nylon brush	brocha plastica	BROH-chah PLAH-stee-kah
oatmeal	avena	ah-VEHN-ah
oats	avenas	ah-VEHN-ahss
octopus	pulpo	POOL-poh
office	oficina	oh-fee-SEE-nah
oil	aceite	ah-say-EE-tay
oily	aceitoso	ah-say-EE-TOH-so
ointment	unquento	oon-KEHN-toh
olive oil	aceite oliva	ah-say-EE-teh oh-LEE-bah
olives	olivos	oh-LEE-vohss
omelette	tortilla	tohr-TEE-yah
on the table	en la mesa	ehn lah-MEH-sah
onion soup	sopa de cebollas	SOH-pah day say-BOH-yahss
onions	cebollas	say-BOH-yahss
orange (color)	anaranjado	ah-nah-rahn-HAH-doh
orange juice	jugo de naranja	HOO-goh day nah-RAHN-yah
orange	naranja	nah-RAHN-hah
oregano	oregano	oh-ray-GAH-noh

ounce	onza	**OHN-sah**
out of order	no funcióna	**noh foon-see-OHN-ah**
outside	afuera	**ah-F*WHERE*-ah**
oven cleaner	detergente para horno	**day-tehr-HEN-tay PAH-rah OHR-noh**
oven	horno	**OHR-noh**
oven racks	parrilla de horno	**pah REE-yah day OHR-noh**
overtime	horas extras	**OHR-ahss ES-trahss**
owner	dueño	**DWEHN-yoh**
oysters	ostras	**OH-strahss**
paint	pintura	**peen-TOO-rah**
paintings	pinturas	**peen-TOO-rahss**
pan	sartén	**sahr-TEHN**
pantry	despensa	**dess-PEN-sah**
pants	pantalones	**pahn-tah-LOH-nehss**
papaya	frutabomba	**froo-tah-BOHM-bah**
paper hats	sombreros papeles	**sohm-BREH-rohss pah-PEH-lehss**
paper napkins	servilletas papeles	**sehr-vee-YEH-tahss pah-PEH-lehss**
paper	papel	**pah-PEHL**

paper towel	toalla papel	toh-AH-yah pah-PEHL
paprika	pimentón	pee-men-TOHN
parchment paper	papel para hornear	pah-pehl PAH-rah ohr-neh-AHR
parking lot	playa de aparcamiento	PLAH-yah day ah-pahr-kah-mee-EHN-toh
parsley	perejil	peh-reh-HEEL
parsnip	chirivía	chee-ree-VEE-ah
partition	división de cuarto	dee-vees-ee-OHN day KWAHR-toh
pasta	pasta Italiana	PAHSS-tah ee-tah-lee-AH-nah
pastry (small)	pastelillo	Pahss-tah-LEE-yoh
pastry	pastalería	pahs-tah-lah-REE-ah
pay	paga	PAH-gah
paymaster	pagador	pah-gah-DOHR
peas	guisantes	ghee-SAHN-tehss
peach	melocotón	meh-loh-coh-TOHN
peanuts	cacahuetes	kah-kah-H*WAY*-tehss
pears	peras	PEH-rahss
pedestal	peana	peh-AH-nah
peeler	cuchillo para pelado	koo-CHEE-yoh PAH-rah peh-LAH-doh

pepper (black)	pimienta	**pee-mee-EN-tah**
pepper shakers	pimienteros	**pee-mee-ehn-TEHR-ohss**
perch	perca	**PEHR-kah**
pheasant	faisán	**faih-SAHN**
photographer	fotografo	**foh-toh-GRAH-foh**
pickles	salmueras	**sahl-M*WHERE*-ahss**
picnic	merienda campestre	**mehr-ee-EN-dah kahm-PEHSS-tray**
picture frame	marco	**MAHR-koh**
pie	pastel	**pahss-TEHL**
pig	cerdo	**SEHR-doh**
pigeon	paloma	**pah-LOH-mah**
pigs' feet	pies de cerdo	**PEE-ess deh SEHR-doh**
pineapple	piña	**PEE-nyah**
pint	pinta	**PEEN-tah**
pitcher	jarra	**HAH-rrah**
placemats	tapetes de mesa	**tah-PEH-tehs day MEH-sah**
plants	plantas	**PLAHN-tahss**
plastic bag	saco plastico	**SAH-koh PLAHSS-tee koh**

plastic pitcher	jarra plastica	HAHR-ah PLAHSS-tee-kah
plastic wrap	papel plastico	PAH-pel PLAHSS-tee-koh
plate	plato	PLAH-toh
plum	ciruela	see-roo-EH-lah
plumber	plómero	PLOH-meh-roh
plumbing	fontanería	fohn-tahn-ah-REE-ah
plunger	émbolo	EHM-boh-loh
poison	veneno	behn-EH-noh
police	policía	poh-lee-SEE-ah
pomegranate	granado	grah-NAH-doh
popcorn	rosetas	roh-SEH-tahss
pork (roast)	cerdo asado	SEHR-doh ah-SAH-doh
pork	carne de cerdo	KAHR-nay day SEHR-doh
pork chop	chuleta de cerdo	chew-LEH-tah day SEHR doh
pork sausage	longaniza	lohn-gahn-EE-sah
port (wine)	oporto	oh-POHR-toh
porter	portero	por-TEH-ro
pot (coffee)	cafetera	kah-feh-TEH-rah

pot (tea)	tetera	teh-TEH-rah
pot	olla	OH-yah
pot soap	jabón para ollas	hah-BOHN PAH-rah OH-yahss
potato chips	papas fritas	PAH-pass FREE-tahss
potato (sweet)	camote	kah-MOH-teh
potato(baked)	papa horno	PAH-pah OHR-noh
potatoes (mashed)	papas molidas	PAH-pahss moh-LEE-dahss
potatoes	papas	PAH-pas
pound	libra	LEE-brah
powdered sugar	azucar en polvo	ah-SOO-kahr ehn POHL-voh
prawn	gamba	GAHM-bah
prep table	mesa para preparación	MEH-sah PAH-rah preh-pah-rah-see-0HN
prep cook	cocino del preparación	koh-SEE-noh day preh-pah-rah-see-OHN
prostitute	ramera	rah-MEHR-ah
prune	ciruela pasa	see-roo-EH-lah PAH-sah
pudding	budín	boo-DEEN
purée	puré	pooh-RAY
purple	purpúreo	puhr-PUHR-ay-oh

quail	codorniz	koh-DOHR-neess
quart	cuarta de galón	KWAHR-tah day gah-LOHN
quince	membrillo	mehm-BREE-yo
rabbit	conejo	koh-NAY-hoh
radiator	radiador	rah-dee-ah-DOHR
radio	radio	RAH-dee-yoh
radish	rabano	RAH-bah-noh
rags	trapos	TRRAH-pohss
raisin	pasa	PAH-sah
raspberries	frambuesas	frahm-BWEH-sahss
rat	rata	RAH-tah
rat trap	trampa para las ratas	TRRAHM-pah PAH-rah lahss RAH-tahss
raw	crudo	KROO-doh
recipe	receta	reh-SEH-tah
record player	tocadiscos	toh-kah-DEES-kohs
red cabbage	repollo rojo	reh-POH-yoh ROH-hoh
red snapper	paigo rojo	pah-EE-goh ROH-hoh
red wine	vino rojo	VEE-noh ROH-hoh

refrigerator	refrigerador	ray-frig-ehr-ah-DOHR
regulations	reglamento	ray-glah-MEN-toh
relative	pariento	pah-ree-EHN-toh
relish	condimento	kohn-dee-MEHN-toe
reservationist	secretario de reservación	seh-kreh-TAH-ree-oh day reh-*sair*-vah-see-OHN
restaurant	restaurante	rehss-toor-AHN-tay
rhubarb	ruibarbo	rroo-ee-BAHR-boh
rice	arroz	ah-RROHSS
right (opp. left)	derecha	deh-RAY-chah
rind	cáscara	KAHSS-kah-rah
rinse	enjuáguelo	ehn-HWAH-gay-loh
ripe	maduro	mah-DOO-roh
roast (roasted)	asado	ah-SAH-doh
roaster (spit)	asador	ah-sah-DOHR
roll (bread)	panecillo	pahn-eh-SEE-yoh
rope	cuerda	K*WHERE*-dah
rosemary	romero	roh-MEH-roh
rubber gloves	guante caucho	GWAHN-teh KOW-choh

rug	alfombra	ahl-FOHM-brah
rum	ron	rohn
Russian dressing	salsa rusa	SAHL-sah ROO-sah
rye bread	pan de centeno	pahn day sehn-TEHN-oh
rye	centeno	sen-TEH-noh
saffron	azafrán	ah-ssah-FRAHN
salad bowl	ensaladera	ehn-sah-lah-DEH-rah
salad	ensalada	ehn-sah-LAH-dah
salad oil	aceite para ensalada	ah-seh-EE-teh PAH-rah en-sah-LAH-dah
salad plates	platos de ensalada	PLAH-tohss day ehn sah-LAH dah
salmon	salmón	sahl-MOHN
salt	sal	sahl
salt and pepper	sal y pimienta	sahl ee pee-mee-EHN-tah
salt shakers	saleros	sahl-EHR-ohss
salty	salado	sah-LAH-doh
sandwich	sándwich	SAHND-weech
sardine	sardina	sahr-DEE-nah
sardine (in can)	sardina en lata	sahr-DEE-nah en LAH-tah

sauce pan	cacerola	kah-seh-ROH-lah
sauce	salsa	SAHL-sah
saucers	platillos	plah-TEE-yohss
sausage	salchicha	sahl-CHEE-chah
saute pans	sartenes	sahr-TEHN-ess
sawdust	aserrín	ah-seh-RREEN
scallions	cebollina	say-boh-YEE-nah
scallops	escalopes	ess-kah-LOH-pehss
schedule	horario	oh-RAH-ree-oh
scissors	tijeras	tee-HEHR-ahs
scouring pads	brillo	BREE-yoh
scraper	raedera	rah-ay-DEHR-ah
screwdriver	destornillador	dehs-tohr-nee-yah-DOHR
seaweed	yerba marina de mar	YEHR-bah mah-REE-nah day mahr
security guard	guardia de seguridad	gahr-DEE-ah day seh-HOO-ree dahd
seeds	pepitas	peh-PEE-tahss
sesame oil	aciete de sesame	ah-seh-teh day SEH-sah may
shad	aloze	ah-LOH-say

shallots	cebollitas	say-boh-YEE-tahss
shark	tiburón	tee-boo-ROHN
shelf	estante	ehs-TAHN-tay
shell	concha	KOHN-cha
shellfish	mariscos	mah-REES-coh
sherbet	sorbete	sohr-BEH-teh
sherry	jerez	HEH-ress
shirt	camisa	kah-MEE-sah
shoes	zapatos	sah-PAH-tohss
short	bajo (a)	BAH-hoh (hah)
shower	dulca	DOOL-kah
shrimp	camarones	kah-mah-ROH-nehss
sick	enfermo	ehn-FEHR-moh
side door	puerta lateral	P*WHERE*-tah lah-TEH-rahl
silverware	los objetos de plata	lohss oh-BEH-tohss day plah-tah
silence	silencio	see-LEHN-see-oh
sink	sumidero	soo-mee-DEHR-oh
sink (kitchen)	fregadero	fray-gah-DEHR-oh

simmer	hervir a fuego lento	EHR-veer ah F*WAY*-goh LEHN-toh
sirloin	solomillo	soh-loh-MEE-yoh
sister	hermana	ehr-MAH-nah
skin (peel)	hollejo	hoh-YEH-hoh
skinny	delgado (a)	del-GAH-doh (dah)
skirt	falda	FAHL-dah
slicing machine	máquina para rebanando	MAH-kee-nah PAH-rah reh-bah-NAHN-doh
slippery	resbaladizo	rehss-bahl-ah-DEE-soh
slow	tardo	TARH-doh
small	pequeño (a)	peh-KEHN-yoh (yah)
smoke alarm	alarma de fuego	ah-LAHR-mah day F*WAY*-goh
smoke	humo	OO-moh
snake	culebra	koo-LEH-brah
snail	caracol	kah-rah-KOHL
snow shovel	pala para nieve	PAH-lah PAH-rah nee-YEH-bay
soap	jabón	hah-BOHN
sober	sobrio	soh-BREE-oh
socks	soda	SOH-dah

sole	leguado	leh-GWAH-doh
son	hijo	EE-hoh
soup plates	platos de sopa	PLAH-tohss day SOH-pah
soup	sopa	SOH-pah
soup spoons	cucharas de sopa	koo-CHAH-rahss deh SOH-pah
sour	agrío	ah-GREE-oh
sour cream	crema agría	KREH-mah ah-GREE-ah
soy sauce	salsa china	SAHL-sah CHEE-nah
spatula (metal)	espatula (metal)	ehs-PAH-too-lah meh-TAHL
spatula (rubber)	espatula (goma)	ehs-PAH-too-lah GOH-mah
speakers (stereo)	bocinas	boh-SEE-nahss
special of the day	plato del día	PLAH-toh dehl DEE-ah
spice	espicia	ess-PEE-cee-ah
spinach	espinaca	ess-pee-NAH-kah
sponge	esponja	ess-POHN-yah
spoon	cuchara	koo-CHAR-ah
sprain	esquince	ess-KEEN-say
squash	calabaza	kah-lah-BAH-sah

squid	calamar	kah-LAH-mahr
staircase	escalera	ess-kah-LEH-rah
statue	estatua	ess-TAH-chew-ah
stale	pasado (a)	pah-SAH-doh (dah)
steak	tajada	tah-HAH-dah
steak sauce	salsa para la tajada	SAHL-sah PAH-rah lah tah-HAH-tah
steam table	mesa de vapor	MEH-sah day vah-POHR
steamed	hervido	ehr-VEE-doh
step (of stairs)	grado	GRAH-doh
stew	guisado	ghee-SAH-doh
stock pots	ollas para caldo	OH-yahss PAH-rah KAL-doh
stomach	estómago	ess-TOH-mah-goh
stool (bar)	taburete	tah-boo-REH-tay
storage room	almacén	ahl-mah-SEHN
stove	estufa	ess-TOO-fah
strainers	coladores	koh-lah-DOHR-ehss
strawberries	fresas	FRAY-sahss
straws	pajas	PAH-hass

stringbeans	habichuelas	hah-bee-CHWAY-lass
stuffed	tofado	toh-FA-doh
sugar	azúcar	ah-SOO-kahr
sugar bowls	azucareras	ah-soo-kah-REHR-ahss
Sunday	domingo	doh-MEENG-goh
sunflower seeds	semilla de girasol	seh-MEE-yah day hee-RAH sohl
supper	cena	SEH-nah
supplies	suministro	soo-mee-NEESS-troh
sweet	dulce	DOOL-seh
swordfish	serucho	seh-ROO-choh
syrup	jarabe	hah-RAH-beh
table cover	sobremesa	soh-breh-MEH-sah
table linen	mantelería	mahn-teh-leh-REE-ah
table	mesa	MEH-sah
table service	servicio de mesa	sehr-VEE-see-oh day MEH-sah
table wine	vino de mesa	VEE-noh day MEH-sah
tablecloth	mantel	mahn-TEHL
tablespoon	cuchara	koo-CHAH-rah

tail	cola	KOH-lah
tall	alto (a)	AHL-toh (tah)
tangerine	mandarina	mahn-dah-REE-nah
tape player	grabadora	grah-bah-DOHR-ah
tarragon	tarragón	tah-rah-GOHN
tarragon vinegar	vinagre tarragón	bee-NAH-*gray* tah-rah-GOHN
taste	gusto	GOO-stoh
tavern	taberno	tah-BEHR-noh
taxi-cab	taxi	TAHK-see
tea (cup of)	taza de té	TAH-sah day tay
tea bags	saco de té	SAH-koh day tay
tea cup	taza para té	TAH-sah PAH-rah tay
tea pot	tetera	teh-TEH-rah
teaspoon	cucharilla	koo-cha-REE-ah
telephone	teléfono	teh-LEH-foh-noh
television	televisión	teh-leh-vee-see-OHN
thick	grueso	grew-EH-soh
thin	fino (a)	FEE-noh (nah)

thirsty	sediento	seh-dee-EHN-toh
Thursday	jueves	H*WAY*-bess
thyme	tomillo	toh-MEE-yoh
time card	carta de punchar	KAHR-tah day poon-CHAR
time clock	reloj de tiempo	reh-LOH day tee-EHM-poh
tin plate	plato lata	PLAH-toh LAH-tah
toast	tostada	tohss-TAH-dah
toaster	toastador	tohss-tah-DOHR
toe	dedo del pie	DEH-doh dell-PEE-eh
toilet paper	papel hygienico	pah-PEHL ee-he-EN-ee-koh
toilet	retrete	ray-TREH-tay
tomato paste	pasta de tomate	PAH-stah day toh-MAH-tay
tomatoes	tomates	toh-MAH-tehss
tongs	pinzas	PEEN-sahss
tongue	lengua	LEN-gwah
toothpicks	palillos	pah-LEE-yohss
towel	toalla	toh-AH-yah
train station	estación de tren	eh-stah-see-OHN day trehn

train	tren	trehn
tray	bandeja	bahn-DEH-hah
tripe	tripa	TREE-pah
trout	trucha	TROO-chah
truck	camión	kah-mee-OHN
tuna	atún	ah-TOON
turkey breast	pechuga de pavo	peh-CHEW-gah day PAH-voh
turkey	pavo	PAH-voh
turnip	nabo	nah-BOH
turtle	tortuga	tohr-TOO-gah
typewriter	máquina de escribir	MAH-kee-nah day ehs-krih-BEER
uncle	tío	TEE-oh
upstairs	piso de arriba	PEE-soh day ahr-REE-bah
urinal	orinal	ohr-ee-NAHL
urinal mints	mentas del orinales	MEHN-tahss dehl ohr-ee-NAHL-ess
vacuum cleaner	aspiradora	ah-spee-rah-DOHR-ah
valet	criado	kree-AH-doh
vanilla	vainilla	bah-NEE-ya

veal	ternera	tehr-NEHR-ah
vegetables	vegetales	beh-jeh-TAH-lehss
veranda	galaría	gah-lah-REE-ah
vestibule	recibidor	ray-see-bee-DOHR
video machine	máquina para video	MAH-kee-nah PAH-rah bee-DEH-oh
vinegar	vinagre	bin-AH-gray
vintage wine	anada	ah-NAH-dah
vomit	vomíto	voh-MEE-toh
wages	salario	sah-LAH-ree-oh
waiter	camarero	kah-mah-REH-roh
waitress	camarera	kah-mah-REH-rah
waitress station	estación de camarera	eh-stah-see-OHN day kah-mah-REH-rah
walk-in box	cuarto frío	KWAHR-toh FREE-oh
walk-in freezer	cuarto helado	KWAHR-toh eh-LAH-doh
wall	pared	pah-REHD
wallet	cartera	kahr-TEH-rah
walnut	nuez	new-EHZ
washing machine	máquina lavadora	MAH-kee-nah lah-vah-DOHR-ah

wastepaper basket	cesto	SEHSS-toh
water	agua	AHG-wah
water chestnut	castaña de agua	kah-STAHN-yah day AHG-wah
water cooler	alcarza	ahl-KAHR-sah
water glasses	vasos de agua	VAH-sohss day AH-gwah
watercress	berro	BEH-rroh
watermelon	sandía	sahn-DEE-ah
wax beans	cera habas	SEH-rah AH-bahs
wedding cake	dulce de boda	DOOL-seh day BOH-dah
wedding	casamiento	kah-sah-mee-EHN-toh
wet	mojado	moh-HAH-doh
wheelchair	silla rodante	SEE-yah roh-DAHN-tay
when	cuando	KWAHN-doh
white	blanco	BLAHN-koh
white bread	pan blanco	pahn BLAHN-koh
white wine	vino blanco	VEE-noh BLAHN-koh
wild duck	pato salvaje	PAH-toh sahl-VAH-heh
window(s)	ventana(s)	ven-TAH-nah(ss)

wine buckets	cubo para vino	KOO-boh PAH-rah VEE-noh
wine cellar	cantina	kahn-TEE-nah
wine glasses	vasos de vino	VAHSS-ohss deh VEE-noh
wine list	lista de vinos	LEE-stah deh VEE-nohss
wine	vino	VEE-no
wooden spoons	cuchara de madera	koo-CHA-rah deh mah-DEHR-ah
yard	yarda	YAHR-dah
year	año	AHN-yoh
yeast	levadura	leh-vah-DOO-rah
yellow	amaríllo	ah-mah-REE-oh
yes	sí	SEE
yoke	yema	YAY-mah
zucchini	calabacitas italianas	kah-lah-bah-SEE-tahs ee-tah-lee-AH-nahss

GLOSSARY

GLOSSARY

Kitchen Spanish

The Beginning to the End
of Language Gridlock
in the Professional Kitchen.

Common Words and Phrases
Simple Instructions
Complex Sentences
Weights & Measures
Numbers - Colors - Times

The Most Complete
Culinary Glossary Anywhere

FITS RIGHT IN YOUR POCKET!

ISBN 0-9651901-0-2

5 1195
9 780965 190107

NEW! UPDATED VERSION

IF YOU CAN READ ENGLISH...
YOU CAN SPEAK...

Kitchen
Spanish

A Quick Phrase Guide of Kitchen and Culinary Terms

Michael A. Friend & T.J. Loughran